HIS
DYING
REQUEST

HIS
DYING
REQUEST

*A Collection of Classic Writings and
Sermons on the Lord's Supper*

BY

DAVID DUNLAP

Published by Bible & Life Ministries, Inc.
1st Edition, January 2006

Bible & Life Ministries, Inc.
David Dunlap
3116 Gulfwind Drive
Land O' Lakes, FL 34639
(813) 996-1053
daviddunlap@earthlink.net

ISBN # 0-9671088-1-0

Printed in the United States of America

CONTENTS

PREFACE

It has been said that worship is the missing jewel of the evangelical church. The Lord's Supper is the most important expression of that worship. This booklet is an effort to take a jeweler's lamp and shine light upon the neglected jewel of worship and the Lord's Supper.

Many great preachers have been burdened by this neglect and have sought to make a difference. Charles Haddon Spurgeon of London (1834-1892) met with a group of godly believers each Lord's Day to celebrate the Lord's Supper. The subject of the Lord's Supper was a frequent theme in his preaching. A Spurgeon biographer, Arnold Dallimore, wrote, "Spurgeon placed great emphasis on the communion service. He made it a time of remembering Christ, especially Christ in His death…he was often so moved that he could barely speak, his voice rich with emotion, and his eyes flowed plentifully with tears."[1] Many of God's choicest servants have had the same commitment to the Lord's Supper as C. H. Spurgeon had.

This collection of classic writings and sermon excerpts on the Lord's Supper is reproduced here to stir believers to spiritual worship. In many cases the sermon excerpts and writings have been slightly altered from their original form. The desire of the editor has been to produce a more readable text. In the chapter by F. W. Krummacher, a chart and a paragraph have been added to clarify the author's point. In the sermon excerpt by H. A. Ironside, its original source is unknown to the editor; therefore, no documentation is noted at the end of that chapter.

In these sermon excerpts, the author's intent, message, or doctrinal viewpoint has in no case been altered. It has been our sincere desire to reproduce these chapters in the same spirit and manner that they were written. We trust that this book might lead you to a greater worship of Christ at the Lord's Supper.

Endnotes

1. Arnold Dallimore, *C. H. Spurgeon,* (Chicago, IL: Moody Press, 1984), p. 197.

FOREWORD

It is a pleasure for me to write this foreword for this book compiled by my friend, David Dunlap. He has a deep concern over the neglect of the Lord's Supper in many churches. This neglect is seen in the formalism and ritual accompanying this service in some churches. The truth that it is a memorial has been perverted into a sacrament, a mystical channel of divine grace, flowing through the emblems themselves.

Because the unregenerate mind does not appreciate the cross work of Christ, the Lord's Supper may be appended to a preaching service and given little emphasis. The goal may be to attract the "unchurched" and to have a service pleasing to them. This means loud "contemporary music," accompanied by a band with a short, inoffensive message following. In some places it is conducted as a separate service in a smaller room with few attending. Because there is little exercise of heart to participate, the service may be programmed in advance.

The purpose of this book is to call Christians back to the importance of this time of worship. It was a vital part of the weekly gathering of the Lord's people in the first century (Acts 2:42; 20:7). This is a plea for the reverent participation of the saints as they function as priests in worshiping (1 Peter 2:5). This requires walking with the Lord throughout the week.

May the Lord use this book to stir the hearts of God's people to worship the Lord "in the beauty of holiness." "For the Father is seeking such to worship Him" (John 4:23 NKJV).

Donald L. Norbie
Greeley, Colorado
2005

1

SPIRITUAL REVIVAL AND THE LORD'S SUPPER

BY DAVID DUNLAP

In the early church, the Lord's Supper was integral to the life of the church. The Lord's Supper was instituted by the Lord Jesus Christ in the gospels. The book of Acts lists the Lord's Supper as one of the four foundational practices of New Testament church life (Acts 2:42). The apostle Paul declares that his teaching on the Lord's Supper was received by special revelation from the risen Christ (1 Cor. 11:23). The weekly Lord's Supper was significant in the life of the early church; it played a central role during the Protestant Reformation in Europe; it was important during the Wesleyan revivals in England. In virtually every major period of church history, the Lord's Supper stood at the forefront of the life of the local church. Throughout the history of the church, whenever the church was experiencing spiritual revival, the Lord's Supper was especially vibrant and alive. However, when the church was in spiritual decline, the worship of Christ at the Lord's Supper was stifled, muted, and shrouded in mystery. In every generation the Lord's Supper functioned as a spiritual barometer, measuring the spiritual health of the church. However, the practice of the Lord's Supper has fallen on unfortunate times. To many believers, the Lord's supper is considered an incidental ordinance of the church to be dispensed with quickly at the end of a preaching service; to others it is an ancient ceremony whose meaning is hidden in mystery and ritual. However, this was not always the case.

THE PURPOSE OF THIS BOOK

This book sets forth the importance of the Lord's Supper through the testimony of history and the preaching of former church leaders. In it you will find articles, quotations, and portions of sermons from respected men of God, such as C. H. Spurgeon, of the Metropolitan Tabernacle in London, and H. A. Ironside, of Moody Memorial Church in Chicago. In their teaching on the Lord's Supper you will not find the arcane theories of men, but rather the heartfelt exaltation of Christ and the New Testament doctrine of the Lord's Supper. It is our hope that these short meditations will stir your heart to re-examine the teaching of Scripture concerning the Lord's Supper, and in doing so, you will be better equipped to worship in spirit and truth.

THE CURRENT SITUATION
IN THE EVANGELICAL CHURCH

Today, as never before, the biblical practice of the Lord's Supper stands in jeopardy. There are many who are questioning its significance. Others are trivializing its importance. Some allege that the regular celebration of the Lord's Supper is an obstacle to church growth. They contend that Scripture never commands us to celebrate the Lord's Supper weekly. Long accepted principles of biblical worship are now being replaced by modern marketing techniques. Clever numerical growth strategies using sociological and demographic studies are competing with the standards and patterns of the Word of God. Saddest of all, in many New Testament churches, the Word of God is losing this all-important battle. If the pages of Christian history could speak, they would raise their uncompromising disapproval. Was there ever a true revival where there was not a return to true worship? Was there ever a time that the practice of the Lord's Supper was not a mark of genuine revival? Would we dare neglect to examine our own spiritual condition when the worship of Christ at the Lord's Supper no longer attracts our hearts? Can our hearts remain unmoved and indifferent when churchgoers crowd in to hear a rock band and drama presentation at the 11:00 service, while there are so few true worshippers found at the Lord's supper? Has the church exchanged holiness and reverence in worship for the atmosphere and glitter of Hollywood? Have we become so busy being happy that we have forgotten to be holy worshippers?

THE 1ST CENTURY CHURCH
AND THE LORD'S SUPPER

The early church period was characterized by spiritual worship. During the first century, after the death of Christ, the church expanded at a rapid rate. Hundreds of local churches were established in Europe, Africa, and throughout Asia Minor. Nevertheless, the Lord's Supper remained central in the life of the local church. Justin Martyr (120-165AD) was a leading historian and apologist for the early church. He describes the vigor and the importance of the Lord's Supper during this time of spiritual revival. He writes,

We greet one another with a holy kiss. Then a leader from the believers takes a loaf of bread and a cup of wine; after taking them, he offers up praise to the Father of all things, through the name of the Lord. When he has ended his prayers and thanksgiving, the whole congregation present assents by saying 'amen.' After thanksgiving, the deacons among us distribute it to those who are present ... no one is allowed to partake of it unless he believes ... For the apostles delivered in the memoirs compiled by them, which are called Gospels, that this command was given to them — that Jesus took bread.[1]

PROTESTANT REFORMATION
AND THE LORD'S SUPPER

During the Reformation many truths that had been shrouded in darkness since the early days of the church were recovered. Some of the truths recovered: were solo fide, salvation by faith alone; Solo Scriptura, the word of God is the sole authority of faith and life; and solo gratis, salvation is by and through the grace of God. However, the New Testament teaching concerning the Lord's Supper was also a leading truth during the Reformation. Thousands of men and women who had found faith in Christ sought to express their worship at the Lord's Supper. One of the leaders of the Reformation, John Calvin, sought to give direction to these swelling numbers of new believers. He wrote in his *Institutes*,

> *At least once a week the table of the Lord ought to be spread before each congregation of Christians, and the promises should be declared for their spiritual nourishment; no person ought to be compelled to partake, but all ought to be exhorted and stimulated, and those who were negligent should be reproved.* [2]

Martin Luther also provided important teaching to these believers. Luther, along with John Calvin and the other Reformers, argued for a weekly remembrance of the Lord's Supper. Historian Scott Brenner writes of Luther's passion concerning the Lord's Supper and its lasting effect on generations of Christians,

> *Luther heartily advocated a return to the Lord's Supper as the normal worship of the congregation on the Lord's Day. The determination of Luther to retain the Lord's Supper as the norm of worship was so strong that the Lutheran churches in Germany continued without a break to worship in this historic way until about 1722, when the acids of rationalism had eroded their biblical moorings.* [3]

The passion for the worship of Christ would not die in Europe with the rise of German Rationalism. In England, the Wesleyan revival would restore some of its New Testament character.

THE WESLEYAN REVIVAL
AND THE LORD'S SUPPER

In every great spiritual revival, renewed emphasis and interest in the Lord's Supper was God's stamp of approval upon that movement. Interest in the Lord's Supper was never a detriment to spiritual growth. Worshipful appreciation of Christ is the natural outflow of a changed heart and life. The most powerful spiritual awakenings in history have often been characterized by a two-fold renewal in worship: firstly, a renewal of simplicity in the practice of the Lord's Supper; then a renewal of spiritual appreciation for the Lord's Supper.

Simplicity of worship has often been a great characteristic of true revival down through the centuries. Elaborate ceremony and arranged worship will, almost without exception, lead to dead ritual, which neither pleases God nor satisfies the heart of man. A true mark of spiritual revival time and again has been a return to worship in simplicity and the rejection of the forms and ceremony of the established churches. The Wesleyan revival in England is a striking example of this practice. The Spirit of God began to work in the hearts of a small company of believers. As they studied God's Word, they were convinced that these principles of worship should be put into practice. In simplicity they attempted to carry out what they found in the Scriptures to be true. Soon the power of God began to change the hearts and lives of these men. As their lives changed, their hearts were soon burdened to express their worship of Christ. Soon, to celebrate the Lord's Supper simply as the New Testament instructs, became their passion. One researcher writes of how the Lord led in their lives,

> *In November, 1729, four young gentlemen of Oxford, Mr. John Wesley, Mr. Charles Wesley, Mr. Morgan, and Mr. Kirkham of Merton College spent some evenings together in reading chiefly the Greek New Testament. To the original four, others were added to the Club, one of whom, John Clayton, son of a Manchester bookseller, led the members in a new direction. In his father's shop he had read many of the early Christian writers and was constantly illuminating discussions with references from the same. Soon the group eagerly embraced the early church practice of the weekly Lord's Supper. The evangelical revival quickly became a revival of worship as well. Hundreds of eager converts crowded into their once near-empty parish churches to receive communion often, to the consternation of the religious leaders who were unused to such enthusiasm. The evangelical leadership was quick to restore, first monthly, and then weekly communion services.* [4]

The simple way of worship also found its way into the life of believers in the north of Great Britain. Fifty-eight years later in Scotland, James and Robert Haldane, ministers of the gospel, traveled in a carriage and were well supplied with tracts which they themselves wrote, printed, and distributed. They spoke in churches and schools, but chiefly in the open air. Hundreds, and sometimes thousands, gathered to hear them; there was much power in their testimony and many were converted. At the fair at Kirkwall, three to four thousand listened daily, and on the Lord's Day some 6,000 gathered to hear. Following the principle of the New Testament, they began to take the Lord's Supper the first day of each week.

Robert Haldane recalled,

I began practicing the Lord's Supper monthly. Afterwards I became convinced that on the principles I held, that I ought to observe it weekly. I met with a few individuals who erected themselves into a church; and I am convinced that any group of Christians may act as we did. [5]

Missionary Revivals
and the Lord's Supper

An accompanying hallmark to simplicity in worship has been a great heartfelt appreciation of Christ at the Lord's Supper. A leading feature of spiritual revival has been the tenderhearted affection present in remembering the Lord Jesus Christ in His death. In America the gospel went forth to the Indians in New Jersey through the missionary David Brainerd. Here, and in other places, as the Spirit of God mightily moved in the hearts of men, spiritual revival was accompanied by a sincere appreciation of the Lord's Supper. David Brainerd wrote in his journal on July 13, 1746,

There appeared tender affection in the assembly under divine truth; my soul was also somewhat refreshed. I administered the Lord's Supper to 31 of the Indians. God seemed to be real

16

and present among us. The worshippers were sweetly melted and refreshed. Oh, how they melted when the elements were first uncovered. There was scarcely a dry eye among them when I took off the linen, and showed them the symbols of Christ's body. [6]

This renewed appreciation of the Lord's Supper was not unique to North America or Great Britain, but was also present in the mission fields of South America. After a number of months of preaching the gospel to Indians in the Ecuadorian jungle, missionary Jim Elliot had seen a small band of believers gather together as a New Testament church. As they began to grow in grace and spiritual maturity, the desire to remember the Lord in His death began to burn in their hearts. Jim Elliot wrote in his journal on January 16, 1955,

With a small nucleus of baptized believers we began having a simple meeting for the breaking of bread, Christ was exalted and worshiped. No one taught; the words of men were few. Hymns of adoration were sung, prayer was offered, and gradually the new believers began to understand the meaning of worship — offering to the Lord the love of their hearts, with simplicity and sincerity. Others began to observe this gathering from the outside. There was not much to watch. The room where we met was the schoolroom—bamboo walls and floors, thatched roof, backless benches. A small table stood in the center of the circle with a loaf of bread and a cup of wine. The Indians gathered quietly, and sat barefooted and reverent around the symbols which spoke to them of the death of their Lord Jesus, whom they had so recently come to know and love. One by one the young men would take part, suggesting a hymn, or praying, while all joined in lifting their hearts to Christ. Reminded of His death, they also thought of His coming again, and frequently ended the meeting singing "Be happy, believers — Christ is coming." [7]

It is refreshing to see Christ-centered worship at the forefront of the gathering-together of the New Testament church. This worship pleases the heart of God and empowers the evangelical witness and spiritual life of the church.

WORSHIP, THE TRUE MARK
OF SPIRITUAL VITALITY

Throughout the centuries, the weekly practice and the genuine appreciation of the Lord's Supper was an indication of the spiritual strength of the Christian church. The past is the great interpreter of the present and a safeguard of the future. A worshipping assembly is always a spiritually robust assembly. Biblical orthodoxy leads to worshipful doxology. Where there is no vision the people perish; and likewise it is true where there is no worship believers languish. When the assembly gathers together, the Lord Jesus Christ must have the first place in all things. He is the Lord of our lives and Head over the church, His body. Unfortunately, today we are beginning to see a marked departure from this essential truth. May the church soon realize that the sincere appreciation and the regular practice of the Lord's Supper is a measure of her spiritual strength. The pattern is plain throughout history: when the church began to forget the Lord in worship, very soon thereafter she also forgot her calling in the world. When we ignore the voice and testimony of history, we do so at our peril.

Endnotes
1. Justin Martyr, *Apology addressed to Emperor Antoninus Pius,* translated by L. W. Bernard, (Cambridge, 1967), p. 61.
2. John Calvin, *The Institutes of Christian Religion,* vol. 2, (Grand Rapids, MI: Eerdmens, 1962), p.602.
3. Scott Brenner, *The Way of Worship,* (New York, NY: MacMillian, 1944), p. 75.
4. Donald Bridge and David Phypers, *Communion: The Meal That Unites,* (Wheaton, IL: Harold Shaw Publishers, 1981), p. 124.
5. E. H. Broadbent, *The Pilgrim Church,* (London: Pickering and Inglis, Ltd, 1931), p. 298, 301.
6. Jonathan Edwards, *The Life of David Brainerd,* (Grand Rapids, MI: Baker Book House, 1978), p. 280.
7. Elisabeth Elliot, *Shadow of the Almighty,* (New York, NY: Harper and Row Publishers, 1956), p. 222.

2

THE WEEKLY REMEMBRANCE OF THE LORD'S SUPPER

BY C. H. SPURGEON

Charles Haddon Spurgeon (1834-1892) was the minister of the Metropolitan Tabernacle in London for 38 years. He is known as the "Prince of preachers." His writings and printed sermons have been a source of rich blessing to many.

Blood represents suffering; but it goes further, and suggests suffering unto death. "The blood is the life thereof," and when blood is too copiously shed, death is suggested. Remember that in the sacred supper you have the bread as a separate emblem of the body, and then the wine as a separate symbol of the blood: thus you have a clear picture of death, since the blood is separated from the flesh. "As often as ye eat this bread, and drink this cup, ye do show the Lord's death." Both acts are essential.

A REMEMBRANCE
OF CHRIST'S SUFFERINGS

Upon the death of Christ you are invited to fix your attention, upon that only. In the suffering of our Lord unto death, we see the boundless stretch of His love. "Greater love hath no man than this, that He lay down His life for His friends." Jesus could not be more loving than to yield Himself unto death, even the death of the cross. O my Lord, in Thy bloody sweat, and in the piercing of Thy hands, and feet, and side, I see the highest proof of Thy love! Here I see that Jesus "loved me, and gave Himself for me." Beloved, I beg you to consider often and lovingly the sufferings of your Redeemer, unto the pouring out of His heart's blood. Go with Him to Gethsemane, and thence to the house of

19

Caiaphas and Annas, and then to Pilate's hall, and Herod's place of mockery! Behold your Lord beneath the cruel scourges, in the hands of the executioners upon the hill of shame. Forget not one of the sorrows which were mingled in the bitter cup of His crucifixion and its pain, its mockery, its shame. It was a death reserved for slaves and felons. To make its deep abysses absolutely bottomless, He was forsaken even of His God. Let the darkness of "Eloi, Eloi, lama sabachtani," bear down upon your spirit till, as you sink in awe, you also rise in love. He loved you better than He loved Himself! That means love, even to the shedding of His blood for you.

The vital importance of the great truth of the death of Christ as a vicarious sacrifice is set before us in this cup, which is the memorial of His blood shed for many. It means something more. We have called our Lord, in our hymn, "Giver of life for life," and that is what this cup means. He gave up His life that we might live. He stood in our place and stead in the day of Jehovah's wrath, receiving into His bosom the fiery sword which was unsheathed for our destruction. The pouring out of His blood has made our peace with God. Jehovah made the soul of His only-begotten an offering for sin, that the guilty might be cleared. "He hath made Him to be sin for us, who knew no sin; that we might be made the righteousness of God in Him." That is what the wine in the cup means: It means the death of Jesus in our stead. It means the blood poured out from the incarnate Son of God made fellowship with God possible for those who were once separated by sin.

Our blessed Savior would have us hold His death in great reverence: it is to be our chief memory. Both the emblems of the Lord's Supper set forth the Savior's death. This peculiarly Christian ordinance teaches nothing if it does not teach this. Christ's death for men is the great doctrine of the church. We profess ourselves partakers of the merit of His death when we come to this table; our Lord's death is then remembered, shown, declared, testified, and trusted in. Evidently the Lord Jesus means us to treat the fact of His death as a truth to be made prominent: He would not have instituted an ordinance specially to remind us of the shedding of His blood, if He had not regarded it as the forefront of His whole earthly career. The other ordinance of our holy faith also sets forth our Lord's death. Are we not "Buried with Him by baptism into death?" Is not baptism an emblem of being immersed beneath the waves of sorrow and death? Baptism shows us that participation in Christ's suffering by which we begin to live; the Lord's Supper shows us that participation in Christ's suffering by which that life is sustained. Both institutions point to His death.

THE DEATH OF CHRIST
IS THE WEIGHTIEST ARTICLE OF FAITH

Besides beloved, we know from Holy Scripture that this doctrine of the death of Christ is the very core of Christianity. Leave out the cross and you have killed the religion of Jesus. Atonement by the blood of Jesus Christ is not an arm of Christian truth; it is the heart of it. Even as the Lord said of the animal, "The blood is the life thereof," so it is true of the gospel; the sacrificial death of Jesus is the very heart of our profession. I know nothing of Christianity without the blood of Christ. No teaching is healthy which throws the cross into the background. The other day, when I was enquiring about the welfare of a certain congregation, my informant told me that there had been few additions to the church, although the minister was a man of ability and industry. Furthermore, he let me see the reason for failure, for he added, "I have attended there for several years, and during all that time, I do not remember hearing a sermon upon the sacrifice of Christ. The atonement is not denied, but it is left out." If this be so, what is to become of our churches? If the light of the atonement is put under a bushel, the darkness will be dense. In omitting the cross you have cut the Achilles tendon of the church: it cannot move, nor even stand, when this is gone. Holy work falls to the ground: it faints and dies when the blood of Jesus is taken away. The cross must be put in the front more than ever by the faithful, because so many are unfaithful. Let us endeavor to make amends for the dishonor done to our divine Master by those who deny or dishonor His vicarious sacrifice: let us abide steadfast in this faith while others waver, and preach Christ crucified if all else forbear. Grace, mercy, and peace be to all who exalt Christ crucified!

THE LORD'S SUPPER IS
A WEEKLY REMEMBRANCE

This remembrance of the death of Christ must be a constant remembrance. The Lord's Supper was meant to be a frequent feast of fellowship. It is a grievous mistake of the church when the communion is held but once in the year, or once in a quarter of a year; and I cannot remember any Scripture which justifies once in the month. I should not feel satisfied without breaking bread on every Lord's Day. It has come to me even oftener than once a week; for it has been my delight to break bread with many a little company of Christian friends. Whenever this Supper is celebrated, we declare that "Christ died for our sins according to the Scriptures." We cannot think of that death too often. Never was man blamed in heaven for preaching Christ too much; nay, not even on earth to the sons of God was the cross ever too much spoken of. Outsiders may say, "This man harps only upon one string." Do you wonder? The carnal mind is enmity against God, and it specially shows its hatred by railing at the cross. Saintly ones find here, in the perpetual monotony of the cross, a greater variety than in all other doctrines put together. Preach you Christ, and Christ, and Christ, and Christ, and nothing else but Christ, and opened ears shall find in your ministry a wondrous harmony of linked sweetnesses, a charming perfectness of all manner of delicious voices. All good things lie within the compass of the cross; its outstretched arms overshadow the whole world of thought; from the east even unto the west it sheds a hallowed influence; meanwhile, its foot is planted deep in the eternal mysteries, and its top pierces all earth-born clouds, and rises to the throne of the Most High. Christ is lifted up upon the cross, that He may draw all men unto Him; and if we desire to draw them, this must be our magnet.

Beloved, the precious blood of Christ should be kept by us in vivid remembrance. There is something to me most touching about that cup filled with the fruit of the vine. The bread of the Supper is the bread of our common meal, and the wine is the usual attendant of feasts. That same pure blood of the grape which is set on our sacramental table I drink with my friend. Look at those ruby, ruddy drops, suggesting your Lord's own blood. I had not dared to invent the symbol, nor might any man of mortal mold have ventured on such a thing, lest he should seem to bring that august death down to our lowly level; but in infinite condescension Jesus Himself chooses the symbol, and while by its materialism He sets forth the reality of the sacrifice, by its commonness He shows how freely we may partake thereof. He would not have us know Him after the flesh, and forget the spiritual nature of His griefs; but yet He would have us know that He was in a real body when bled, and that He died a real death, and became most truly fit for burial; and therefore He symbolizes His blood, not by some airy fancy, or mystic sign, but by common wine in the cup. Thus would He reach us by our eye and by our taste, using two gates of our nature which lead up to the castle of the heart. O blessed Master, by what striking methods do You teach us? Then let us be impressed with the reality of the lesson, and never treat Thy passion as a thing of sentiment, nor make it a myth, nor view it as a dream of the imagination. Thou shalt be in death most real to us, even as is that cup whereof we drink. The dear memorials of our Lord's blood-shedding are intended for a personal remembrance. There is no Lord's Supper except as the wine touches the lip, and is received into the Christian's own self. All must partake of it. He says "drink ye all of it." You cannot take the Lord's Supper by deputy or representative; you must each of you approach the table, and personally eat and drink. Beloved, we must come into personal contact with the death of Christ. This is essential. We must each one say, "He loved me, and gave Himself for me." In His blood you must be personally washed; by His blood you must be personally reconciled to God; through His blood you must personally have access to God; and by His blood you must personally overcome the enemy of your souls. As the Israelite's own door must be smeared with the blood of the Passover lamb, so must you individually partake of the true Sacrifice, and know each one for himself the power of His redemption.

REMEMBRANCE IS MARKED BY SINCERE WORSHIP

As it is personal, it is a charming fact that it is a happy remembrance. Our remembrance of Christ is chastened with repentance, but it is also perfumed with faith. The Lord's Supper is no funeral meal, but a festival; most fitly do we begin it with the giving of thanks, and close it with a hymn. It is by many called the "Euchrist," or the giving of thanks: it is not a fast, but a feast. My happiest moments are with the king at His table, when His banner over me is love. The death of Christ is a well spring of solemn joy. Before our great Sacrifice died, the best token of His death was the blood of bulls and of goats. See how the victims writhe in death! The sacrificial knife does terrible work at the foot of the altar; it is hard to stand by, and see the creatures bleed. After our Lord's death was over, the blood of animals was not the type, but the blood of the grape. That which was terrible in prospect is joyous in remembrance. That which was blood in the shedding is wine in the receiving. It came from Him with a wound, but it comes to us in a blessing. His blood is our song in the house of our pilgrimage and it shall add the best music to our heavenly harmonies as we sing before the throne: "Unto Him that hath loved us, and washed us from our sins in

His own blood; to Him be glory for ever and ever." If our Lord Jesus has made the memory of *His love* to be more sweet than wine, let us never turn from it as though it had become a distasteful theme. Let us find our choicest pleasures at the cross.

A MEMORIAL OF CHRIST'S CHANGELESS REDEMPTION

Once more, our Savior meant us to maintain the doctrine of His death, and the shedding of His blood for the remission of sins, even to the end of time, for He made it to be of perpetual remembrance. We drink this cup "until He come." If the Lord Jesus had foreseen with approval the changes in religious thought which would be brought about by our advancing "culture," *He* would surely have arranged a change of symbols to suit the change of doctrines. Would *He* not have warned us that, towards the end of the nineteenth century, men would become so "enlightened" that the faith of Christendom must of necessity take a new departure, and therefore He had appointed a change of sacramental memorials? But *He* has not warned us of the coming of those eminently great and wise men who have changed all things, and abolished the old-fashioned truths for which martyrs died. Brethren, I do not believe in the wisdom of these men, and their changes I abhor; but had there been any ground for such changes, the Lord's Supper would not have been made of perpetual obligation. The permanence of ordinances indicates a permanence of doctrine. But hear the moderns talk—"The Apostles, the Fathers, the Puritans, they were excellent men, no doubt, but then, you see, they lived before the rise of those wonderful scientific men who have enlightened us so much." Let me repeat what I have said. If we had come to a new point as to believing, should we not have come to a new point as to the ordinances in which those beliefs are embodied? I think so. The evident intent of Christ in giving us settled ordinances, and especially in settling this one which so clearly commemorates His blood shedding, was that we might know that the truth of His sacrifice is forever fixed and settled, and must unchangeably remain the essence of his gospel. Neither nineteen centuries, nor nineteen thousand centuries, can make the slightest difference in this truth, nor in the relative proportion of this truth to other truths, so long as this dispensation lasts. Until He comes a second time without a sin-offering unto salvation, the grand work of His first coming must be kept first and foremost in all our teaching, trusting, and testifying. As in the southern hemisphere the cross is the mariner's guide, so, under all skies, is the death of our Redeemer the polestar of our hope upon the sea of life. In life and in death we will glory in the cross of Christ; and never be ashamed of it.

Endnotes

C. H. Spurgeon, *A Treasury of Spurgeon, The Blood Shed for Many,* (Grand Rapids, MI: Baker Books, 1979), pp.33-38.

3

REVERENCE IN THE LOCAL ASSEMBLY

BY DAVID DUNLAP

"Holy, holy, holy is the Lord of hosts; the whole earth is full of His glory! . . . for mine eyes have seen the King, the Lord."

— Isaiah 6:3, 5

The spiritual condition of Israel demanded a fresh and powerful manifestation of God's holiness. The holiness of God had gripped Isaiah's heart with unusual power and conviction. He was humbled by Him who is exalted high above all His creatures with infinite greatness. He saw, like never before, that there was a great chasm between the holiness of God and the sinfulness of man. Therefore, Isaiah unfolds to his people the holiness of God unlike any other prophet before him.

ISRAEL'S SPIRITUAL CONDITION

King Uzziah had reigned in Judah for 52 years. This king had protected his people from its enemies and brought a measure of economic prosperity and a sense of security. Inwardly, however, the nation was morally corrupt, spiritually empty, and superficial in its worship of God. As a result, in Isaiah chapter 5, Isaiah pronounces six judgments of woe upon Judah. Many in Judah believed that they were in a proper spiritual condition because of their economic prosperity. But in 740 B.C. King Uzziah died of leprosy when God struck him down because of his pride. When Uzziah died, the nation's sense of security was shattered, and Isaiah sensed the need to enter into the presence of God. It was here that God gripped Isaiah with an awesome sense of His presence and holiness. He saw the Lord high and lifted up. He heard the seraphim cry back and forth, "Holy, Holy, Holy, is the Lord of Hosts, the whole earth is filled with His glory" (6:3). He is broken by his own unworthiness. Why was Isaiah so visibly shaken by all that he had seen and heard? He tells us the reason, "mine eyes have seen the King, the Lord of Hosts" (Isa. 6:5).

Likewise, when we are gripped by the holiness of God, our instant and only reaction must be worship and reverence. Without such a revelation or conviction, we cannot truly worship God. Holiness and reverence are the life-blood of worship. Worship that is marked by a fresh vision of God's holiness is never casual, flippant, and superficial. True worshippers do not rush into His holy presence unprepared to bow in reverence. Sincere worshippers of God possess deep convictions about the holiness and glory of God. A. P. Gibbs explains,

> *Spiritual tone is difficult to describe, but is nevertheless very real and can be readily discerned by spiritual believers. There is a sense of the presence of God, of the reality of the unseen, but eternal, verities, and the hush of reverent awe, that quiets the spirit and prepares the soul for worship.* [1]

However, just as in Isaiah's day there was great spiritual apathy, so also is there much spiritual indifference and casualness in the church today.

The Need for Reverent Worship

Many are concerned that today there is too much shallowness in our worship of God. Irreverence in worship is now becoming all too common in modern churches. Unfortunately, New Testament assemblies are not immune to this affliction. Increasingly, believers are sauntering into worship meetings 10 to 15 minutes late, without the slightest hint of embarrassment. The retelling of personal anecdotes, the singing of favorite hymns, and nonchalance have replaced holy and reverent worship. Psalm 111:9 exhorts, "Holy and reverend is His Name." Hearts full of Christ have now given way to hearts full of competing interests.

Many still attend times of worship, but have lost their first love. The stirring hymns of the faith are still sung, but rarely with passion and conviction. Gripping passages of Scripture about Christ and the cross are still read, but with little apparent devotion or heart-felt affection. Eloquent prayers of praise and worship ring hollow.

TRUE REVERENCE

It was not always this way. In earlier days, the assemblies were known for men of God whose passion to worship the Son of God was unrivaled. The believers in the Lord Jesus Christ might have gathered in a grange hall or a refurbished building, but the gathering place was not as important as the gathering Center, the Lord Jesus Christ. The hymns were sung heartily. Worship was mingled with tenderness and devotion by men of God who knew the Word of God. There was a beauty of holiness that attracted all true saints of God. The holiness and reverence that characterized the meeting was evident to all. Concerning the character of those meetings, one writes,

> *I sometimes smile when I hear ministers state the assumption that a new type of building will create a worship atmosphere. In my late adolescence I occasionally worshiped with those known as "Plymouth Brethren." Meeting in the barest halls, adorned only with signs carrying Scripture verses, they had the most worshipful services that I have ever attended. No organist in whispering conferences, pushing or pulling stops. Greeting, giggling, whispering, and coughing were all hushed by the miracle drug: reverence. Children were quieted. People tiptoed to their places in the circle to sit with bowed heads or read their Bibles. The keen anticipation of the movement of the Spirit of God in leading one of the assembled men to announce a hymn, read the Scripture, or to offer prayer was sensed in these moments of deep reverence, which sharply contrasts with the hubbub of many protestant services.[2]*

Reverence is not something we can bring to God or create in ourselves; but rather, it is a spiritual grace we receive when we begin to see God as He truly is. Reverence acknowledges in our hearts the glory of God as presented in the Scriptures, and then yields to God His rightful place in our lives. Reverent worshippers acknowledge their unworthiness and, in godly fear, bow before an awesome and holy God. Concerning this source of holy reverence, the Swiss reformer John Calvin writes,

> *Reverence is that dread and amazement with which holy men were struck and overwhelmed whenever they beheld the presence of God. . .Men are never duly touched and impressed with a conviction of their insignificance, until they have contrasted themselves with the majesty of God.*[3]

Just a sudden glimpse of the holiness of God will change us forever. As Isaiah is thrust into the presence of God and the seraphim cry out, "Holy, holy, holy," the prophet confesses, "Woe is me! For I am undone." Isaiah, the righteous prophet, in one brief moment, is exposed and broken under the gaze of the Almighty. In an instant, he is measured by the ultimate standard of holiness; he is weighed in the balance and is found wanting. The holiness of God has seized his heart, soul, and mind. He cannot forget what he has seen. Boredom, casualness, and lukewarmness about the things of God are gone for ever. "Mine eyes have seen the King, the Lord of Hosts" (Isa. 6:5).

THE BIBLICAL STANDARD
FOR REVERENT WORSHIP

All too frequently, churchgoers who have never had a fresh vision of God's holiness gather to worship God. Nice songs are sung, religious thoughts are offered to God, and well-crafted words are uttered; but all this falls far short of true worship. This worship may be more psychological and fleshly than spiritual. This kind of worship bears no resemblance to the worship that we find in Scripture. The psalmist writes, "He is to be feared above all gods . . . splendor and majesty are before Him, strength and beauty are in His sanctuary . . . O worship the Lord in the beauty of holiness: fear before Him all the earth" (Ps. 96:4,

6, 9). Godly fear, majesty, the beauty of holiness, and splendor were ready themes of the worshippers of old. There are many who study theology, but where are those who are studying to be worshippers of God? Where are the churches today whose primary focus is to "worship God in spirit and truth"? A. W. Tozer exhorted the church prior to his death in 1963,

Many of our popular songs and choruses in praise of Christ are hollow and unconvincing. Some are even shocking in their amorous endearments, and strike a reverent soul as being a kind of flattery offered to One with whom neither composer nor singer is acquainted. The whole thing is in the mood of a love ditty, the only difference being the substitution of the name of Christ for that of the earthly lover. How different and how utterly wonderful are the emotions aroused by true and Spirit-incited love for Christ! Such love may rise to a degree of adoration almost beyond the power of the heart to endure, yet at the same time it will be serious, elevated, chaste, and reverent. Christ can never be known without a sense of awe and fear accompanying the knowledge. He is the fairest among ten thousand, but also the Lord high and mighty. He is the friend of sinners, but also the terror of devils. He is meek and lowly in heart, but He is also the Lord and Christ who will surely come to be the judge of all men. No one who knows Him intimately can ever be flippant in His presence. If Bible Christianity is to survive the present world upheaval, we shall need to recapture the spirit of worship. [4]

A CALL TO REVERENT WORSHIP

Sadly, reverence seems to be strangely absent within the evangelical church. Worship, the Lord's Supper, and the great doctrines concerning Christ no longer seem to grip us. These do not seem to be popular. We are a spiritually carefree generation. Sadly, the broad road has always been more appealing than the narrow way. Nevertheless, let us draw near unto Him, who in mercy first drew near to us, and humbly bow our hearts as worshippers in the presence of the sovereign Head of the church, the

Lord of Glory. May our reverent worship to Christ once again shine brightly as the hallmark of our devotion to Christ.

Endnotes

1. A. P. Gibbs, *Worship,* (Kansas City, KS: Walterick, 1980), p. 216.
2. John W. Drakeford, *The Awesome Power of a Listening Heart,* (Grand Rapids, MI: Zondervan, 1985).
3. R. C. Sproul, *The Holiness of God,* (Wheaton, IL: Tyndale House, 1985), p. 72.
4. A.W. Tozer, *That Incredible Christian,* The Art of True Worship, (Harrisburg, PA: Christian Publications, 1964), p. 125.

4

THE CENTRAL FOCUS OF THE LORD'S SUPPER

BY H. A. IRONSIDE

This article was adapted from a sermon given by Henry Allan Ironside (1876-1951). He was internationally beloved for his teaching of the Word of God. He ministered at Moody Memorial Church, in Chicago for over 20 years and labored in the exposition of the Scripture for over 50 years. He was the author of over 60 books.

The last Passover feast that God ever recognized was that celebrated by Jesus Himself, with His disciples, in the guest chamber at Jerusalem. On that same evening, He instituted the great central ordinance of Christianity, the Lord's Supper, the memorial of His mighty love and infinite sacrifice. Directions for the keeping of this feast are clearly given in the New Testament. Believers, who have gone on in the ways of Christ, should always be able to give a scriptural reason for everything connected with the observance of the breaking of the bread in remembrance of the Lord Jesus Christ. It is my desire, as simply as possible, to attempt to answer some of the questions regarding the Lord's Supper, having in mind older, but also new, believers in Christ who desire to walk in obedience to His Word.

THE FREQUENCY OF THE LORD'S SUPPER

Perhaps one of the first questions that will be asked is, "Why observe this feast so frequently when, in many places, it is only at rare intervals that what is commonly called 'the communion' is celebrated?" We reply that we have, in Scripture, no distinct commandment as regarding the particular times it is to be celebrated. The Passover was celebrated once per year, but, when the Lord instituted the Supper, He implied much more frequent observance when He said, "As often as you do this, do it in remembrance of Me." It is the Lord's desire that His people often show His death in this way, calling to mind frequently His love and sacrifice for them. In the earliest days of the church's history, the Christians broke bread daily; but, when the first days of transition passed, and the new dispensation was fully established, we get the Scriptural example in Acts 20:7, "Upon the first day of the week the disciples came together to break bread and Paul preached unto them."

In apostolic days, it is well-known that this was the recognized custom. Now this is not a commandment, but it is a word from the Lord, and He has said, "If a man love Me he will keep My words." A devoted heart does not ask "How seldom can I do this and yet have the Lord's approval?," but "What does His Word tell us about the established order in the early days?" The book answers, "On the first day of the week," and, therefore, upon that day, we delight to come together to remember Him.

No Officiating Clergy

"But when so coming together," the question is asked, "why is there no officiating clergyman to dispense the elements and take charge of the service, as is done in the denominations around us?" We answer, because we cannot find anything like that in the Book. There is no intimation anywhere, either in the Acts or in any of the epistles, of any such officer of the church. Believers came together as brethren. The Lord Himself has said, "Where two or three are gathered together in My name, there am I in the midst" (Matt. 18:20). Faith laid hold of that and recognized His presence. He, the Head of the assembly, is today as true to His Word as in the early days. Wherever two or three are found scripturally gathered, He is in the midst to take charge by the Holy Spirit and to lead out the hearts of His people in their remembrance of Himself. Of old, in that upper room, when the time came to break the loaf and pass the cup, His own lips pronounced the blessing, and His own hands gave to His disciples. Christ is now in heaven. But Christ's church embraces the Lord Jesus Christ as Head, and its believers on earth as members of His Body. Just as He used the members of His literal body of old to bless and give the emblems, so now He uses the members of His body, the church, as it may please Him. Any brother going to the table to give thanks and to break the loaf or pass the cup becomes, for the moment, hands and lips for the blessed Lord. There is no human officialism required; the simpler the better. It is Christ with Whom we desire to be occupied. If anything more were necessary, the pages of Scripture would somewhere indicate it to us, but in regard to this we search in vain. "One is your Master, even Christ, and all ye are brethren" (Matt. 23:8).

THE MEANING OF
THE LOAF AND THE CUP

"Why do you have one unbroken loaf upon the table at the beginning, and why is it broken afterwards?" Because the one loaf pictures the precious body of our Lord Jesus Christ in its entirety and the breaking signifies His death. Also we are told, "We being many are one loaf (bread), for we are all partakers of that one loaf" (1 Cor.10:16-17). To cut the bread into small pieces, as is sometimes done, is to lose sight altogether of this striking symbolism. As it is passed from one to the other, after having been blessed and broken, each again breaks for himself, thus indicating his communion with the body of Christ. "What is in the cup, and why do all drink of it?" The cup contains the fruit of the vine. It speaks of the precious blood of Christ, the price of our redemption. "The cup which we bless is it not the communion of the blood of Christ?" Just as the rich clusters of grapes are cast into the wine-press and pressed to give forth what Scripture calls the "blood of the grape" (Deut. 32:14), so Christ endured the judgment of God for our sins; and when He suffered on the

35

cross, His precious atoning blood flowed for our salvation. As we drink in silent worship, we recall, with grateful hearts, the mighty cost of our redemption.

CHRIST THE CENTRAL FOCUS
OF THE LORD'S SUPPER

"Why is there no previously-arranged program as to the order of service, the hymns to be sung, prayers to be offered, and the words of heart-felt worship? Is not time wasted in silence which might be used in teaching the Scriptures?" It is important, first of all, to understand that we do not come together to pray, or yet to preach, or to sing or listen to teaching, or to enjoy Christian fellowship. We come together to meet the Lord Himself, to be solely occupied with Him, to offer Him the worship of our hearts, and to remember what He passed through for us. Let me put it this way: Suppose that on a given Lord's Day morning it were known definitely that our Savior, in person, would be present in our church building. How do you think real Christians would act on such an occasion? Would we not enter the room with a deep sense of awe pervading our spirits? Surely there would be no lightness of behavior, no frivolity, no worldly jesting as we came together. Nor would we be coming to listen to one preaching or teaching the Word of God. Our one desire would be to see Him, to fix our adoring eyes upon His blessed Face; if we spoke at all, it would be to tell something of His sufferings for us, and the gratitude and worship that would fill our hearts as we recalled the agony He endured on the cross. At such a time, one can well understand how all might join in a burst of melody, singing together some hymn of praise, in which His holy person, His past sufferings, and His present glory were celebrated! But surely anything like mere fleshly formalism would be altogether out of place. If one spoke audibly, it would be simply to praise His Name, or to bring to the mind of saints some portion of the Word that would give a better understanding and apprehension of His person or work. No one would dare to push

Christ aside, and take His place as the teacher of others, unless requested by the Lord.

THE LORD'S SUPPER AND SPIRIT-LED WORSHIP

It must be remembered that when we come together for the Lord's Supper, Christ is as truly present in our midst as He was among the first disciples two thousand years ago. Yes, there will be room for praise and for the reading of a portion from the Word of God, which might bring out more vividly the sufferings of Christ. But any brother would be decidedly out of place who sought to give a lengthy exposition of Scripture or an exhortation to the believers. The sense of awe which comes over the soul who recognizes he is in the Lord's presence will curb the flesh. The Holy Spirit will guide those gathered concerning prayers of worship, the spiritual tone, and portions of the Word of God which exalt the Lord Jesus Christ. If there be periods of silence, there will be no wasted time as we all sit gazing with rapt, adoring eyes upon Himself, whom we have come to meet. It is also well understood that prayers of a general nature, prayers for the salvation of the lost, and intercessions for the sick are quite out of place. These subjects of prayer are necessary, proper, and good, but should be brought before the Lord at the weekly prayer meeting and in private prayer.

THE LORD'S SUPPER IS FOR TRUE CHRISTIANS

"Why is this holy and reverent time of worship not open for everyone? Why is such care taken so that only true believers and those walking faithfully with the Lord partake at this worship time?" This supper is for those who have a deep love for Christ and have been saved by His blood. In 1 Corinthians chapter 5, Christians are directed to walk in a path of separation from evil and evil-doers. We are told, "with such a one do not eat." Again in 1 Corinthians 6, we have impressed upon us the importance of walking apart from the world, if we are to have fellowship in the things of God. This clearly includes the Lord's Supper, and shows to us its holy character. And while it is true that each individual is responsible to examine himself, before sitting down to eat of the loaf and drink of the cup, there is a grave responsibility resting on assemblies of Christians to maintain a fellowship that is holy and faithful to the instruction of Christ.

A CALL TO REVERENCE
AT THE LORD'S SUPPER

In closing, let me press upon the hearts of the worshipers at the Lord's Supper to remember that distractions during these times can greatly disturb spiritual worship. A little care as to this will often go a long way towards creating a climate for precious and happy times of worship. Sadly, individuals coming in late and distracting the attention of others may greatly hinder the worship of the heart. It is a pitiful commentary on the spiritual state of many believers that they can be sharply on time every weekday morning to their places of business or employment, and yet be among the stragglers on the first day of the week, when the hour set is much later than that which they frequently go to business. A heart for Christ is what is needed to put this right.

5

SURPRISED BY
HIS PRESENCE
BY CHARLES STANLEY

Charles Stanley (1821-1888) was a much-used servant of the Lord in the mid to late 1800's. The following is his account of how he was first introduced, as a young man, to the observance of the Lord's Supper in scriptural simplicity.

Let me tell you about an event that turned the whole current of my future course from that day to this. I had heard that Captain W. and a few other Christians met on the first day of the week to break bread, like the disciples in Acts 20:7. One Lord's Day morning, I went to see what this could mean. I found them gathered in an upper room in Wellington Street, Sheffield. I sat behind, and naturally looked for the pulpit. There was no pulpit, but a table spread, or covered, with a white cloth, and on it the bread and wine, in commemoration of the death of the Lord Jesus. I then looked for the minister, or president. There was no such person. All the believers gathered were seated around the table. A deep, solemn impression fell upon me: "These people have come to meet the Lord Himself." I have no doubt it was the Spirit of God that thus spoke to me. It is impossible to describe the sense I had, for the first time, of being in the immediate presence of the Lord Jesus, according to that word, "For where two or three are gathered together in My name, there am I in the midst of them." I could scarcely notice what was done, I was so overwhelmed with the presence of the Lord. No one can have any idea what this is, unless he is really gathered to His name. What a contrast to everything I had seen before, and yet how simple! It was like going back to that which was in the beginning of Christianity — before any priest was heard of to offer in the church a sacrifice for the living and the dead. I was much surprised to find, strange as this gathering together of Christians to break bread appeared to me, that it was exactly what we find in Scripture. Instead of even a minister at the Lord's Table, I found the same simple liberty as described in 1 Corinthians 14:29-37. I was greatly struck with each believer worshipping the Lord, in dependence on the Holy Spirit. I felt that was my place, deeply unworthy as I was of it. Well do I remember the thought, "This is my place, if even it were to be a doormat, for these Christians to wipe their feet on me."

After some weeks, I was named as one who desired to obey the Lord, "Do this in remembrance of Me," and through grace, I took my place, as one redeemed to God, at the table. Shortly after this, I experienced one morning, while we sat in silent worship, what I had never known before — the leading of the Spirit of God. It came as a gentle whisper from the Lord, "Read 2 Corinthians, chapter 1," and very precious thoughts came into my soul on verses 3 to 5. I felt agitated, so much so that perspiration ran down my face and body. We had sat some time in silence. I felt bidden to rise and read, but had not courage to do so. At length, Captain W., who sat at the other side of the room, arose and said, "Let us read 2 Corinthians 1." Then he ministered the very thoughts the Spirit had laid on my heart. This was how I first learned the leadings of the Spirit in the midst of Christians gathered to Christ. This has been a matter of frequent occurrence for these many years.

Endnotes

Charles Stanley, *Incidents of Gospel Work,* (London: George Morrish, ND), p. 20-23.

6

SPIRIT-LED WORSHIP AND THE LORD'S SUPPER

BY J. B. WATSON

Joseph Barnes Watson (1884-1955) was the long time editor of Witness Magazine, co-author of "On the Sermon on the Mount," and a respected Bible teacher for many years in Great Britain.

"This do in remembrance of Me." Throughout all the world, wherever the Gospel of Jesus Christ has been preached and men and women have come to a knowledge of Christ, there are groups of saved people gathered together in order that they might observe the direction of those words: "This do in remembrance of Me." If a first-century Christian could be transported through all the centuries, and sat down here in our twentieth century as an observer in some of those gatherings, he would not be able in many of them to discern a single feature that had survived since the first century. The original ordinance has been so overlaid with human tradition and priestly assumptions that it has become barely recognizable. But still, it may be held that even now, in this late hour of our dispensation, such an observer could happen upon companies of people who, upon the first day of the week, observe this ordinance in a way that very closely approximates to that with which he himself would have been familiar, away back in New Testament days. First Corinthians 11 gives the divine warrant for the service of the Lord's Supper, and in chapter 20 of Acts we have a New Testament example of a local church meeting together to remember the Lord in the breaking of the bread.

There is surviving to our day a letter from the second century written by Justin Martyr (120-165 A.D.), in which he gives details for the breaking of bread, which differ very little from the New Testament Scriptures. He says,

We all hold this united assembly on Sunday, because that is the first day of the week, in which God turned aside darkness and matter, and made the world, and because Jesus Christ our Savior on that day rose from the dead.

Later in the letter he says,

On the day called Sunday there is an assembly in one place of all the Christians who dwell in the cities or in the country, and the memorials of the apostles or the writings of the prophets, are read as time may permit.

So, when they came together in the second century, they did it on the first day of the week. They came together for the purpose of breaking bread, and they took opportunity in their gathering to minister the Word of God. Now imagine yourself one only yesterday born again, knowing scarcely any thing of Christian doctrine or practice, just as they were in the city of Corinth. Suppose you were to visit such a company of Christians on the first day of the week, and find them seated around a simply-spread table which bears two simple emblems—bread and wine. As the service proceeds, the question arises in your mind; why do they do this? If you were to ask a believer after the service, he might say something like this: "Why, we do it because our blessed Lord asked us to do it. On that very night when His heart was as full of sorrow as it was of love, He looked into the faces of His own that were clustered around Him and said to them with longing in His heart: 'This do in remembrance of me.' " We do it because He asked us to do it." This is really the fundamental answer. You may read books a foot thick on the Lord's Supper, and you will never get beyond this truth. Wonderful it is, after all that the learned men say, to discover that this is still the very heart of the matter. We do it because He said: "This do."

LORD'S SUPPER
AS A MEMORIAL FEAST

Now, there are other reasons why we celebrate the Lord's supper. It is a memorial feast. When we come together around the Lord's table, we come having Himself before our thoughts. At the supper, we turn aside for a time from the demands of business, and family life, and turn our inward gaze upon Christ alone. A hundred and one lawful things fill our thoughts at other hours, but when we take our place at the Lord's table, we empty our hands and minds of all of these, and Christ fills our memory. At the Lord's table, memory functions at its very highest level, for there it occupies itself with our Master and Lord. At the Lord's table, the Holy Spirit is the King's Remembrancer indeed, for He brings the Lord before our souls in all His glory and fullness, from eternal glory to Bethlehem to Calvary and back to His throne in heaven.

At the Lord's table, every eye is fastened on Him. It is a memorial feast. There is still more to the memorial feast. The Lord's Supper is the Lord's divine method to drive us back week by week to the center and heart of our faith: Christ. The Lord, who knows our needs more than we know ourselves, saw how needful it was to bring us back to the very heart, core, and foundation of our faith, again and again. Sunday by Sunday our hearts are set aflame anew by the mighty mystery of Calvary. The world is so full of many voices that might well drive us away from the true center of things; but not many days will pass till the Lord's Day comes anew and we fulfill His wish, and memory, mind, thoughts, and affection are all brought back face to face with the infinite wonder of Calvary's most bitter cross.

CORPORATE PROCLAMATION
OF THE LORD'S DEATH

The Lord's Supper is an announcement, a proclamation, and corporate preaching of the Lord's death. I have heard Christians say, "I can remember the Lord without any rite or ceremony." I have heard Christians who neglect the Lord's table excuse themselves by saying they remember the Lord every day. I hope they do. I am sorry for any Christian who does not. However, the Lord's Supper is so central to the purposes of God that He has decreed and ordained that, in both the dispensation before it occurred and in the dispensation since it occurred, there should be in the world by His people a corporate recognition and proclamation of that mighty event. In Israel year by year, the Paschal feast pointed to the Calvary that was yet to be; and in the church for more than twenty centuries, the Lord's Supper has pointed to Calvary. The church corporately shows forth the Lord's death—the most important event couched between two eternities. The Lord's death; the death that annulled death. The death that drew the sting of death. The one death, since death entered, that was completely voluntary, but also the only death that has ever been undertaken by divine authorization. The death which is life to those who believe on Him. Let no man say that he can neglect the Lord's command: "This do." For it is an ugly perspective in a man's soul when he assumes to be able to get on without something that the Lord has seen necessary to provide. It is also a confession of our hope. "You do show the Lord's death—until He come." You say: "What is it all about, the death that abolished death? You Christians are no different from other people. You still have to attend funerals." But when we are gathered together around the Lord's table, we are saying "wait." We are waiting. The first installment of victory over death is already in glory. We are waiting for the trumpet sound, and the ancient graves will be stirred by His command, and we will meet together in the air, to be forever with the Lord. We are saying with one voice, we are saying to an unbelieving world, we are saying to hostile spiritual powers, we are saying to the reinforcing of each others faith, we are saying to the pleasure of our God and Father, "We do this till He come."

DIVINE BLUEPRINT FOR PARTICIPATION AT THE LORD SUPPER

How should we observe the Lord's Supper? At the very birth of the Church, back in the beginning of the Acts of the Apostles, the Bible says they "broke bread." They continued steadfastly in the Apostles' doctrine, in breaking of bread, and prayers (Acts 2:42). In the twentieth chapter of the Acts, it says, "And we sailed away from Philippi after the days of unleavened bread, and came unto them at Troas in five days, where we abode seven days. And upon the first day of the week, when the disciples came together to break bread Paul preached unto them" (Acts 20:6-7). I want you to notice that, in order to be present when the disciples came together, Paul waited full seven days in Troas. He apparently arrived there on what we would call a Monday morning, and consequently, in order that he should meet all the saints when they came together as was their custom on the first day of the week, he tarried seven days at Troas. When you come together as an assembly, that is, when Christians meet in the capacity of a church, you come together as such on the first day of the week primarily to remember the Lord in the breaking of the bread. They came together as a local church, a church that was formed by the Holy Spirit, to be a witness for Christ in that locality. But that is not all. "The cup of blessing which we bless, is it not the communion of the blood of Christ? The bread which we break, is it not the communion of the body of Christ?" The meaning of these words is simply this: the cup at the Lord's Supper represents the blood of Christ. The bread over which we pray a blessing is a united giving of thanks. When they came together there was a united giving of thanks, for the bread and for the wine. Every Scripture about the Lord's Supper makes this plain, that all Christians present in the Church in a spiritual oneness partook of the bread and the cup. Scripture also teaches that upon coming together the Church took this opportunity to set forth the Word of God for the building up of the body through spiritual gifts that Christ has given to the church.

SPIRITUALITY AND
THE LORD'S SUPPER

Some comment, "You have no priest to administer the sacrament." Look into the Scriptures, and if you find such a person, then all New Testament churches will also have such a person. But you will look in vain, for the Bible never speaks of such a person. The New Testament Greek scholar Dean Alford writes,

The blessing of the cup and the breaking of the bread were not the acts of the minister as by any authority peculiar to himself, but only as the representative of the whole Christian congregation present. The figment of sacerdotal consecration of the elements by transmitted power is as alien from the apostolic writing as it is from the spirit of the gospel.

When a brother rises in this hall some Sunday morning, and gives thanks for the bread, he is only expressing the united thanksgiving of every Christian present. He is not a minister in any other sense than that. One might say, "You do not even have a presiding elder to see that the service is kept in an orderly way." No, we do not. Look in chapter 11 of First Corinthians and find such a person if you can. You will have to put on a very powerful pair of reading glasses to find even the shadow of such a person, and if ever one was needed, it was at Corinth at that time. There was such a state of things at the Lord's table that makes our blood run cold to consider. Drunken hands were being put to the cup of the Lord in Corinth, and if ever it was needful to reduce all this confusion, it was there. Well, how is order to be obtained? The apostle simply reaffirms divine principles to them. That is all. Let the Holy Ghost send home the Word of God to their hearts, and that will reduce chaos to order. Let them bow their wills to the Word of God and seek to be guided by the Spirit of God. Brethren, at the Lord's table, if the Word of God means anything, we have this: the Lord in the midst of us, the Spirit of God within us, and the Word of God behind us. Do we want anymore? It is the Lord's table. That word occurs again and again here. "I have received of the Lord." It was the Lord who, "the same night which He was betrayed, took bread"; and it is the Lord's death that we are remembering. It is the body and blood of the Lord that are before us in symbols, and all through the Bible it is the Lordship of Christ that is emphasized. If only the hearts of God's people understood what it means to have the Lord in the midst, then they will need neither priest nor presiding elder, but they will have sufficiency in the guidance of the Holy Ghost. When I have put together all that is written about the Lord's Supper, I have to notice this: a peculiar absence of any rules; what seems to be a deliberate and designed vagueness as to details. You will not find a word in the New Testament as to the composition of the elements. Bread. Read where you will, it is bread. That is the force and center of the emblem and you do not find any directions about what the wine should be. You find this: the cup. No, the Lord says, "I am not going to have them worrying about the composition of what is in the cup." It is true He once said: "the fruit of the vine." There are some who say that the Lord's Supper must be celebrated in the evening. The Scripture says: the first day of the week. It does not say any more than that. "As often as you eat this bread." Isn't that delightfully free, lifting us above these details? The Lord's method always required that we should have a spiritual mind. When we fall from spirituality, then we begin to make rules, and to bring in human expedients to take the place of the beautiful simplicity and spirituality. You say, "This meeting that seems to have no leader, does it work?" It does this: it calls for constant exercise of heart on the part of the Lord's people, and God wants that from us all the time. If we fall into a routine, then the fall is great, and we all feel it. It means a solemn self-scrutiny before we come to the Lord's Supper. It means a sincere heart and our eye completely upon the Lord. It means that we shall come up in the Spirit, on the Lord's Day. Yes, it means all of that. But thank God it does. These are just the things we need to be kept fresh in, and that we need to be kept falling from.

Now there is nothing whatever in this simple feast that merely pleases the flesh. No. When we come around that table, with its simple emblems, there is nothing there that will please that which is merely sensuous, aesthetic. No peals of thrilling music, no arched temple full of soft light that comes through windows of stained glass, no purple and gold upon the vestments of the priests. No high altar of carved marble, lit with innumerable candles; no incense, filling the whole place with its heavy perfume. Nothing of all of this that is so pleasing to the natural and sensuous aesthetic in man. But it is only in a barn or a cottage kitchen or a simple meeting house, where the two's and three's meet, because He said: "This do in remembrance of Me." These who worship, do so in all dependence upon Him, in all submission to His Lordship, in all sincerity, seeking to be guided by His Holy Spirit; those are hours nearest to heaven. Those are the minutes when the soul realizes the presence of the Lord in a measure beyond all other hours. Then it is that the love of Christ melts our hearts and causes our eyes to overflow. Then it is that we look at the Man of Calvary, and then it is that we stoop and kiss the Conqueror's feet. Then it is that we see afresh the wounded hand and side, and say with Thomas, "My Lord and my God!"

Endnotes

J. B. Watson, *J. B. Watson: Selected Writings,* Lord's Supper, (Great Britain, Gospel Tract Publication, 1988), pp. 137-147.

7

SPIRITUAL PREPARATION FOR THE LORD'S SUPPER

BY HAROLD ST. JOHN

Harold St. John (1876-1959) beloved British expositor. He authored "Analysis of the Gospel of Mark," "Behold His Glory: the Glory of Christ in the Gospel of John." His daughter Patricia, was well known as the author of books for children.

In 1 Corinthians 11:17-34, we have another abuse that was found at Corinth, and again you must remember the customs of the time. Here is what was then called the Lord's Supper and it consisted of a social feast always held at night. The reason was that the bulk of the Christians were slaves, and the only time a slave could get out was after 9 o'clock in the evening when the Master had had his dinner, and he must be back by 5 o'clock in the morning; so once a week they had, for about eight hours, one meeting that covered all the services in the church. They might have a Bible Reading and a bit of ministry, and it commenced with a social meal, a sort of picnic when everybody brought their own food. If that is done in the spirit of love it is a very beautiful thing.

THE LORD'S SUPPER
AND THE "LOVE FEAST"

This meeting began with a communal meal, what the Greeks called a supper basket; the wealthy brethren, men of leisure, came in with a hamper full of the very nicest things, and they sat down. The head of the family got a corner where later hundreds of Christians would be, and he gave thanks and then they started

49

to eat their meal. As the apostle says, "In your eating each one taketh before the other his own supper; and one is hungry and another drunken (11:21)," i.e. the man who came in first with the large hamper has eaten very well and has drunk a good deal more than he ought to have drunk, and perhaps is a little noisy. When the social feast was over they would settle down to have the breaking of bread service, always at the end of the supper. Just as they are getting to the end of the first meal there comes into the room a poor brother, hungry and dusty. He could not even snatch a crust from his master's table. He sees that man with his reddened face and air of jovial enjoyment and he says, look at that man, he might have waited for me and shared his food with me; there comes in a spirit of jealousy and rivalry, and the other one is contemptuous. One takes the best seat in the room and the other, as James puts it, has to sit at his footstool. The jealousy of the poor slave, and the self-indulgence of the rich man are each of them alike canceling out everything for which Christ died. Christ died to make it possible for the wealthy, poor, strong, weak, young, old, Barbarian and Scythian, bond and free to find themselves in a happy fellowship. "All that call upon the name of our Lord Jesus Christ in every place, their Lord and ours." Yet by their actions they are setting up again the barriers that Christ died to break down, forming one Body in which the link should be the life of Christ and the love of Christ. That is the tragic thing, says Paul. He says if you want to make a meal, a really satisfying meal out of this love feast, why don't you have your food before you come? (v. 21), "Have ye not houses to eat and drink in?"; (v. 34), "If any man is hungry let him eat at home," and then come and have spiritual food, not to indulge and gratify his hunger, but just to have an orderly expression of brotherly love, and then pass the bread and wine which tells of the love of Christ.

The Night the Lord
was Betrayed

Look back to the darkest night in this world's history, the night when Jesus Christ was betrayed. There is a question about

v. 23, because the words translated "delivered" and "betrayed" are exactly the same and each means "handed over." In the case of the second "in which He was betrayed" it might mean, as sometimes in the Gospels, the day the Father handed Him over to the will of man, but I think myself that probably "betrayed" is the better rendering here. It might be the treachery that Judas worked, or it might be the Father giving the Son over to death, but we'll leave it with the little reminder that the word is exactly the same in both cases. Now, he says, there was somebody willing to betray the Lord Jesus. Go back in thought to that upper room, the extraordinary heartbreaking grief as those men sat around their Savior while He poured into their hearts the ministry that would be their support for nineteen hundred years of His absence. If you remembered that, could you treat your brethren as you are doing and gratify the lusts of your flesh to the neglect and contempt of your poorer brethren? Go back to the upper room and see how you feel when you think of the place where all your blessings started, "On that night He took the bread: and when He had given thanks He brake it, and said, Take, eat, this is My body which is broken for you: this do in remembrance of Me. In like manner also the cup, after supper, saying, This cup is the new covenant in My blood: this do ye as oft as ye drink it, in remembrance of Me. For as often as ye eat this bread, and drink the cup, ye proclaim the Lord's death till He come." Aren't you thankful that there is nothing said as to how often we should remember the Lord? "As oft as ye do it" says Paul. At the beginning, in the early flush of first love they seem to have broken bread every day. At Troas (Acts 20:7) they broke bread on the first day of the week, and I think that is the seal and sanction for millions of Christians. Whenever you do it you shall have two things before you as far as this chapter is concerned. First, you look back "in remembrance of Me."

THE LORD'S SUPPER
AND GOD, THE FATHER

Then in the next verse, you look forward and "proclaim the Lord's death till He come." The question of the "showing" has often been taken up, and a very old illustration will bring this before us. To whom shall we proclaim it? Surely not to the world. The Supper in its very essence is a private thing. Not to one another, that would not be very gratifying. To the angels you show it because these things the angels desire to look into. But who is the Person in the universe who most appreciates the death of the Christ of God? Imagine on a winter's day there is a sparrow standing on a cornice of a building. It has not eaten, is frozen, loses consciousness, falls and its life is dashed out upon the pavement. Now the Lord said, when the sparrow falls to the ground My Father is there. It does not fall without the Father. God is interested in the death of a sparrow. Then go to Psalm 116:15, "Precious in the sight of the Lord is the death of His saints." If He is interested in the sparrow's death, how much more in the death of a saint, like Stephen for instance, or any one of you. But when it comes to the death of His Son, is there any subject on earth which would so fill the heart of God with tides of feeling than to have that death presented before His eye and heart by the Lord's people. The Person who appreciates it most is the Father who sent the Son to be the Savior of the world. The death of sparrows and of saints, but the death of the blessed Son—what will that mean to God the Father when you show it to Him? And you go on doing it for how long?—until He comes back again!

Personal Preparation
for the Lord's Supper

How are we going to keep ourselves, as the years roll on, from a sense of familiarity, and remember Christ truly and show His death rightly? Paul tells us that we must prepare our hearts so that we do not eat and drink unworthily (11:27). You are going to take bread, by which you identify yourself with the Body of Christ, and take the cup, whereby you affirm your fidelity to the covenant because the cup, we are told, is the new covenant in His blood. (Christ has made that covenant, and every time you lift the communion cup you say by an action and your heart says it in words, I am proclaiming an act of loyalty to a covenant which this cup represents, the death of One Who died to establish the rights of God, "The earth is the Lord's and the fullness thereof" (1 Cor. 10:26). The devil denied that and said the world was his, but Christ died to establish the rights of God, and you say, I stand with Christ when I take the cup, He died to make this covenant by which the demons have been dispossessed and the angels brought in. I am not surprised that Christians are persecuted in many countries, the devil would do it here if he could, you see it is the death sentence to his whole order, as you lift the cup proclaiming "the earth shall be full of the knowledge of the Lord as the waters cover the sea." Each time you break bread you proclaim that you belong to another world, that you are a citizen of another country, bound by a covenant; and it will be the death sentence to the whole order around you. But remember the meaning of the act, you are affirming your loyalty to another Head, not of this world but of another country.) Paul says get into that state of soul that will enable you to look back and remember Him and look forward and cherish the thought of His return. Be very careful that there is not a single thing in your life that casts a shadow on your fellowship with God. Late on Saturday evening I like to go over the week with God and say, Lord, there was this to confess and regret, that opportunity missed, that piece of service done. Get everything behind you in the week that has gone and have the accounts completely cleared up, wrongs put right, for it may not be too late to put it right on Saturday night, but if you can't do it then, do it at the first possible opportunity, and then keep very short accounts with the Lord. With nothing to cause disquiet in your mind, go into the room where the Lord's people are met in assembly, and you are prepared to break the bread and take the cup. There is very little virtue in performing outward acts unless the heart is in tune. If you look back on all that has been going on in the week, say ten minutes after you get into the meeting, you have to waste precious time confessing this thing while your brethren are soaring on wings of faith, enjoying the Lord and tasting the most blessed privilege reserved for us until we get to heaven. You Corinthians, says Paul, are self-indulgent, proud, and envious of each other. Do you ever wonder why a number have died lately, and why there is a great deal of sickness in the meeting? Why did the Lord take them away? Just because they were careless and had taken the Lord's Supper in a loose, and careless fashion.

PERSONAL EXAMINATION
AT THE LORD'S SUPPER

Do not mix this discipline of 1 Corinthians 11 with the discipline of chapter 5. That is man's discipline and perfectly right, "Put out from amongst yourselves that wicked person," i.e. a man fallen into gross sin. But this has nothing to do with the church. The Lord loves you much too well to let you get away with the thing although it is only yourself and the Lord who knows it. And the Lord says even if I have to put you on a sick bed or take you away, the one thing I won't suffer is that you shall eat the bread and take the cup carelessly, unworthily, cherishing thoughts of wrong, selfishness or evil in the heart. Now, says Paul, these are the two things we must get put right. First the outward thing, the matter of dress, but underneath it, the eternal principal of the Headship of Christ, His place in the scheme of creation, the place God has given Him, or "the head of the man is Christ; and the head of the woman is the man; and the head of Christ is God." And all that is involved, says Paul, if you come in carelessly, outraging the spiritual sensibilities of the angels, and secondly, in what state of heart are you going to remember your Lord; how shall you think of Him and how shall you proclaim His death and His coming?

Endnotes

Harold St. John, *The Collected Writings of Harold St. John,* Lord's Supper, (Glasgow, GB: Gospel Tract Publications, 1986), pp. 272-276.

8

THE INSTITUTION OF THE LORD'S SUPPER

BY F. W. KRUMMACHER

Friedrich Wilhelm Krummacher (1796-1868) was one of the most influential ministers in Germany. He was a fierce opponent of liberal modernism in Germany. He is the author of "Elijah, the Tishbite" and "The Suffering Savior." His book "The Suffering Savior" is considered a timeless Christian classic.

The Passover has been kept according to Israelitish practice, the paschal lamb has been consumed by the guests with feelings of deep emotion, and the festive cup has been sent round several times as was customary. The moment had now arrived when, after singing the great "Hallel," (psalm of praise), the meal should be concluded, and the signal given to the guests to rise up and depart. Instead of this, what occurs? The Master, on whom all eyes were directed, rises from His seat, not to leave the room, but to commence a new and still more solemn act than that of eating the Passover. In the capacity of the head of the family, He again takes the bread, breaks it, and after giving thanks, distributes it to His disciples. He then likewise passes them the cup, and commands them all to drink of it.

LORD'S SUPPER
AND THE FOUR GOSPELS

Heaven alone can satisfactorily explain to us why the evangelists have not transmitted to us the words of institution used by the Savior, in perfect agreement with each other as to their form and manner. "But," you say, "Have they not done so?" No, my

55

friends. In Matthew and Mark, the Lord, in breaking the bread, says, "Take, eat, this is My body." According to Paul (1 Cor. 11:24), He used the expression, "Take eat this is My body given for you." In Matthew, he says of the cup, "Drink ye all of it; for this is My blood of the New Testament, which is shed for many for the remission of sins" (Matt. 26:27-28). In Mark, both the words, "Drink ye all of it," as well as "for the remission of sins," are wanting. In Luke, we find the Lord saying, "This cup is the New Testament in my blood, which is shed for you" (Luke 22:20). Paul expresses it in like manner, but describes the Lord as adding, "This do ye, as oft as ye drink it, in remembrance of Me" (1 Cor. 11:25). There are differences in these gospel passages, but there are certainly no contradictions or errors. Now how are these variations in the four narratives to be explained? A variety of explanations, as one may imagine, has been suggested during eighteen centuries of church history. But I must protest, on the outset, against the idea, entertained by many people, that one or other of the evangelists had made a mistake, and was unable to remember the precise words used by the Lord Jesus. The apostles, in compiling their inspired records, were preserved from every error. For their Lord and Master had expressly promised them that the Comforter, the Holy Spirit, should guide them into all truth, and bring all things to their remembrance that He had spoken to them (John 14:26). And we cannot, for a moment, suppose that the Holy Spirit was deficient in such an important matter as the institution of this ordinance, but gave Himself to it with the greatest exactness.

But perhaps you say, "How will you be able to reconcile the differences which really exist?" My readers, I do not for a moment doubt that the Lord uttered all the words which are recorded, and that the four witnesses only enlarge each other's description of what occurred. It is my conviction, that on distributing the bread and presenting the cup He several times uttered the words of institution, repeating them, first in one form and then in another.

THE LORD'S SUPPER
AND 1 CORINTHIANS

Certainly, it is not a matter of indifference to be able to place our foot on firm ground in this matter, and with perfect confidence to say, "These are the original words of institution used by our Lord, in their authentic and proper context. We can be assured of their essential and true meaning, and these are the exact words which are to continue in use forever, according to the will of our Lord Himself." But in order to provide for the real requirements of His Church on earth, the Lord was subsequently pleased to give His apostle Paul a clear revelation concerning the word of the institution of His holy ordinance. Hear what the apostle says in 1 Cor. 11:23, "For I have received of the Lord, that which also I delivered unto you, that the Lord Jesus, on the same night in which He was betrayed, took bread." The substance of the institution is consequently expressed as to the bread, in the words, "This is My body which is broken for you; this do in remembrance of Me;" and as to the cup, in the words, "This cup is the new testament in My blood; this do ye, as oft as ye drink it, in remembrance of Me."

There is something remarkable in this first statement. Paul, who was not present at the institution of the supper, nonetheless supplies the exact words that are recorded in the synoptic gospels. In the first part of the statement given by Paul in 1 Corinthians, we have the words our Lord used in Matthew and Mark, "Take, eat, this is my body." However, in the second part of Paul's statement we have the words recorded by Luke, "which is given for you: do this in remembrance of Me." Therefore, we can be assured that the statement of the apostle Paul, given to him by the resurrected Christ, contains the exact words of the Lord at the institution of the Lord's Supper.

Matt. 26:26	"Take eat, this is my body…"
Mark 14:22	"Take eat this is my body…"
Luke 22:19	"This is my body given for you do this in remembrance of me."
1 Cor. 11:24	Take eat, this is my body which is given for you do this in remembrance of me." (NKJV)

*Figure 1

THE USE OF LEAVENED BREAD AT THE LORD'S SUPPER

Let us now cast a look at the actions with which our Lord accompanied the words. We read firstly that "the Lord took bread." Observe that He took bread, and not the flesh of the Passover lamb; this He did that He might not suggest, in any way, such coarse ideas concerning the bread as those expressed by the Jews at Capernaum (John 6). The bread which He took was the unleavened Passover bread; *however, this was not subsequently used. The first Christians at their communion, which they initially celebrated almost daily, made use of the customary bread; that is, bread that was used at their dining tables, and therefore leavened.*** "The Lord took bread," this most indispensable sustenance, the product of the most valuable of earth's fruits, which presents an extremely striking image of Him without whom we have no spiritual life.

There are those who argue that the bread is not a symbol of the body of Christ, but the actual flesh of Christ. To them I would reply that, then, you must overlook the Lord's words in John, 6:51, "I am the living bread, which came down from heaven, and give life unto the world." The Lord also speaks of the "corn of wheat which falls into the ground," referring to His death, burial, and resurrection (John 12:23). These metaphors were given not to be interpreted literally, but rather to teach spiritual truth.

THE GIVING OF THANKS
AND THE LORD'S SUPPER

After the Lord had taken the bread, He lifted up His eyes toward heaven, and "gave thanks"—that is, He poured out His heart in praise and thanksgiving to His heavenly Father. For what did He render thanks? O my friends, for what else than for the decision of divine mercy, to save such poor sinners as we, which He saw in spirit, as already accomplished in His blood, and for the deliverance of the children of Adam from the curse of the law, the power of Satan, and eternal punishment. It was they who lay continually upon His heart; to whose restoration all His cares and anxieties were directed, and whose exaltation and blessing was the object of His highest interest and hope. He gave thanks. O, with what adoring delight will the holy angels have caught this costly incense in their golden censers and have borne it up to God! He gave thanks. We ought also to give thanks. But it is well for us, that in this, as in everything else, He intercedes for us, and covers our guilt with His death and our deficiencies with His fullness.

After our Lord had given thanks and blessed it, He "broke" the bread. Nor is this without a deeper meaning, as He Himself declares immediately afterward, in the words, "This is My body, which is ("broken" KJV) given for you." In every New Testament book, whether it be the gospels or the writing of Paul, where the institution of this holy ordinance is recorded, they do not fail to record this breaking of the bread. Jesus broke it as symbolic of that which should soon occur to His own body, by which He should become our atoning sacrifice and the bread of life. In the breaking of the bread, He depicted His own death to the eyes of the disciples; and the sublime and admirable tranquility with which He did so, again testifies of the infinite love to sinners which pervaded his heart. Our Lord presented the bread, thus broken, to His disciples, and it is here that we see Him in His proper role and favorite service. Giving, presenting, and communicating, is His delight. As then, so now, His hand is stretched out in His feast of love, although presently hidden in the hand of His human messengers. We, His servants, step back, as regards ourselves, entirely into the background, while distributing the bread and cup. We are then nothing but His instruments. He Himself is always the dispenser and giver. Hence, His words alone are heard at the holy feast; and no other words should be used, no matter how beautiful and believing they may sound.

The Emblem of the Cup
at the Lord's Supper

At the prayer for the cup, the same words were repeated as at the blessing of the bread. After renewed thanksgiving and blessing, our Lord presented the cup to His disciples, and invited them all to drink of it. He calls the wine His blood, even as He designated the bread as His body; and, both elements united, represent the whole Christ, inasmuch as He gave His life, which is "in the blood," unto death, as an atoning-sacrifice for us. That the Lord did not select water but wine for the symbol of His shed blood, was done from the wisest motives. For His words only magnify the glory of Christ, who is the real Vine, and in Whom we possess divine life. In addition, the wine reminds us of the winepress of suffering and sacrifice, in which the Son of God was set forth as our Savior and Mediator. In contrast, the bread represents the body of our Lord who bore sin for our deliverance and redemption.

What an incomparable legacy the Lord left for us in His holy Supper! What a fullness of heavenly blessings and mercies has He showered down upon us in this simple institution! Let us therefore hold this precious feast in high esteem. May we be found in humble worship at His table for the blessing of our inner man. Only let us be careful to appear in His presence clothed with reverence and humility of spirit. As we worship Him, we shall feel more constrained to render heartfelt thanks unto Him, who has bought us with His blood.

Endnotes

* Figure 1. Chart and preceding paragraph is supplied by the editor.

** Italic provided by editor.

Taken from F. W. Krummacher, *The Suffering Savior,* The Institution of the Lord's Supper, (Grand Rapids, MI: Baker, 1977), pp. 53-59

9

CONCLUSION – HIS DYING REQUEST

When men near the end of their lives, they call family and friends to their bedside and with their last dying breaths, they share with them their last words. These words are usually the thoughts and requests that are very important and near to their hearts. When our Lord Jesus Christ instituted the first Lord's Supper it was there that he shared with his disciples His dying request. This last request to His disciples might have been the most important personal charge that He ever gave to them. He said, "With desire I have desired to eat this Passover with you before I suffer;. . . This is my body which I have given for you: this do in remembrance of me."

In Israel of old, the Tabernacle was in the center of the camp, and the dwelling places were arranged outward from that tent north, south, east, and west but all facing toward it. On the altar of burnt offering, the priests offered sacrifices for sin every morning and evening. In so doing, Israelites were reminded of their sin twice every day as the smoke of those sacrifices rose from the center of the camp. It was the Lord's intent that they should be brought face to face with their sin and the sacrifice for it every day. The Lord Jesus Christ in the upper room told His disciples that the church should also have a memorial. However this memorial is not one that is repeated morning and evening, nor is this memorial one that is designed to remind us of our sin, but to remind us of our Deliverer from sin, the Lord Jesus Christ. In this remembrance it was the Lord's intent that we might never forget the infinite work of Christ upon the Cross, and in so doing we might come to bow our hearts weekly in worship and thanksgiving.

There would be no punishment connected to those who out of neglect did not remember Him in worship at the Lord's Supper. He knew that such punishment might bring about frequent worship but not the true worship rising out of a heart of love. This holy place where our Lord requests His people to remember Him, is a place where no flesh can glory, and where Christ alone is magnified. The psalmist doubtless had this in mind when he wrote, "And in His temple doth everyone speak of His glory" (Ps. 29:9). May all sincere Christians re-examine their understanding of the Lord's Supper, and in so doing, may Christ receive the highest worship.

Suggested Reading

Gibbs, Alfred P., *Worship,* (Kansas City, KS: Walterick Press)
Gibbs, Alfred P., *The Lord's Supper,* (Kansas City, KS: Walterick Press)
Tozer, A. W., *Worship: the Missing Jewel of the Evangelical Church,* (Harrisburg, PA: Christian Publications)